the**handbag**

to have and to hold

the**handbag**

to have and to hold

CARMEL ALLEN

CARLTON

THIS IS A CARLTON BOOK

This edition published by Carlton Books Limited 1999
20 St Anne's Court
Wardour Street
London W1V 3AW

A CIP catalogue for this book is available
from the British Library.

ISBN 1 85868 769 1

Printed and bound in Dubai.

Senior executive editor: Venetia Penfold
Art director: Penny Stock
Editor: Lisa Dyer
Designer: Barbara Zuñiga
Picture researcher: Catherine Costelloe
Special photography: Patrice de Villiers
Production: Alexia Turner

A Note from the Author and Publisher

Every effort has been made to include all major handbag
designers, but lack of space has inevitably meant that
some designers have not been included. We apologize
for any omissions and hasten to add that this is in no way
a reflection of the designers' ability.

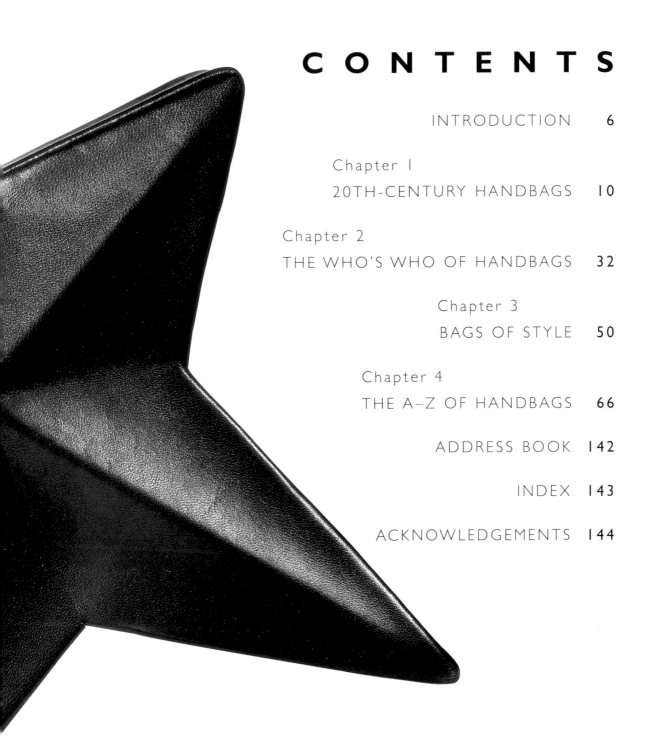

CONTENTS

INTRODUCTION

Not long ago I was at a party where I happened to mention that I was writing a book about handbags. 'I have to confess', said a rather smart woman, 'that I've never carried a picture of my husband and children in my wallet, but', she continued, pulling a small well-thumbed piece of paper from her slim, velvet evening purse, 'I do carry a picture of my dream handbag.' She then showed us a picture of the Hermès Birkin as if it were her first-born. I was not at all surprised by her behaviour; when I lived in Italy I had two girlfriends who put their names down for Kelly bags at the same time so they could share the six months' wait together. It really was as if they were expecting. Some may scoff and snigger, as I did, at their mounting excitement over what is, essentially, a few pieces of leather stitched together in an artful way, but handbags are like cars – some models are vintage while others are classics, but neither is just a means of getting from A to B.

More than just a fashionable accessory, the handbag is chosen by the modern woman in the knowledge that it will become her own private but portable boudoir, office, bank and emergency kit, without which she would undoubtedly feel totally lost. Even the smallest handbag will defy the laws of physics to hold mobile phone, Filofax, Psion organizer, lipstick, mirror and hairbrush, not to mention money, credit cards, keys and the odd mint. The handbag is the lady-in-waiting to the woman who gets by without a chauffeur to drive her and a butler awaiting her arrival at home.

CHAPTER 1

20th-CENTURY HANDBAGS

AS TIMES CHANGE, SO DO HANDBAGS. I REMEMBER MY MOTHER HAVING SEVERAL SMART, SNAP-SHUT BAGS WITH SOFT SUEDE LININGS, WHICH SHE CHOSE ACCORDING TO HER SHOES, THE COLOUR OF HER SUIT AND THE OCCASION. FOR THE EVENING SHE HAD MANY OTHERS, INCLUDING SEVERAL BLACK VELVET CLUTCH BAGS OF VARYING SIZES. SHE WAS OF THE GENERATION THAT GREW UP WEARING HATS AND GLOVES, THAT WOULD NEVER DREAM OF GOING BARE-LEGGED. FOR HER, THE RIGHT HANDBAG WAS DETERMINED BY A COMBINATION OF PURPOSE AND PROPRIETY. EVEN NOW, SHE FINDS THE PAIRING OF A DELICATELY BEADED PURSE WITH TROUSERS OR A MINI RUCKSACK WITH A FLOATY DRESS TO BE FAINTLY RIDICULOUS AND TOTALLY INAPPROPRIATE. WHEREAS FASHION ONCE DICTATED THE RULES – LIKE MATCHING HANDBAGS AND SHOES – IT NOW BREAKS THEM TO MOVE FORWARD. TODAY THERE IS SOMETHING VERY AWKWARD-LOOKING AND DATED ABOUT ALL THOSE PASTEL-CLAD WOMEN AT ASCOT WITH THEIR CAREFULLY PAIRED SHOES AND HANDBAGS. TOMORROW FASHION WILL CHANGE AGAIN, BUT FOR NOW WE CAN LOOK BACK AND ASSESS ALL THE CHANGES THUS FAR.

W omen, it seems, have held the purse strings for a relatively short time. Although the handbag is thought of as an exclusively feminine accessory, the forerunner is the pouches men wore to carry coins in ancient times. In fact, the very words 'handbag' and 'purse' stem from the Latin *bursa* and the Greek *byrsa*, which were used to describe these small bags. Later, the Normans used an *aulmonière*, which came from the word for alms and almoner and referred to a pouch suspended from a girdle worn by men – just think of Robin Hood and the bulging bags of coins robbed from the rich and given to the poor. In the twelfth century the Italians (who else?) created the first 'designer' pouches; leather examples were made by artisans of the Florentine leather-workers guild, while elaborate silk ones were crafted in Venice. In the sixteenth century two important changes took place that enabled women to take the handbag and purse for their own. It became customary for men to give their sweethearts velvet purses containing portraits of themselves and precious keepsakes made from enamel, gems and gold. At the same time, men's clothing changed, with the introduction of wide breeches containing hidden pockets that did away with the need for purses, which had hindered weapon-carrying.

NAUGHTY NINETIES

The last ten years of the nineteenth century were affectionately known as the Naughty Nineties, a reflection of the decline of the stiff Victorian values and the rise of the *belle époque*. Those who had wealth lived extravagant lives, especially the high society in the USA, like the Stuyvesant and Vanderbilt families. Long dresses, elaborate hats and ornate, grand pieces of jewellery were the order of the day, but only for married women. It was still considered bad form for young unmarried women to encourage male attention by dressing up – status and seniority dictated one's dress code. Handbags were bejewelled, embroidered or beaded for evening, with small drawstring Dorothy bags or petite purses with wrist straps being favoured. Clutch bags and shoulder bags were not used until much later. By day, smart but very sober leather handbags were carried, similar to those used by Queen Elizabeth today. The World Fair in Paris in 1900 and the death of Queen Victoria in 1901 heralded new thinking and fresh designs. The *haut monde* and the *beau monde* were to meet. Travel remained important, not just for those working in the colonies, but also for the women who embarked on the grand tour. Luggage was essential, so companies like Louis Vuitton and Hermès flourished. Women needed hat boxes, trunks for their hooped dresses, vanity boxes for their cosmetics and

travel bags that would hold everything they needed during long train or coach journeys. In 1901, Louis Vuitton created the canvas and leather steamer bag and cabin trunk, designed to fit neatly under the beds of transatlantic ships.

THE NEW CENTURY

By the beginning of the twentieth century, women were already hankering after more freedom. Travel and education meant they were no longer happy to be the passive, decorative accompaniment to a male-dominated home and workplace. In 1903 Emmeline Pankhurst founded the Women's Social and Political Union in Britain, and in doing so consolidated the suffragette movement. However, women really began to be treated differently when the First World War broke out in 1914. Their help in the war effort was necessary, and women – even

those from the upper echelons of society – wanted to volunteer. Women of all classes began mixing together and social barriers began to fall. With men at war, women took over jobs that were traditionally in the male domain, and became train drivers, factory workers, land girls and much more. Their clothing changed accordingly, and women began to wear dungarees, trousers, sensible boots, and scarves instead of hats. Bags became utilitarian, like game bags and cartridge bags, satchels and despatch bags, which could be slung over a shoulder while cycling or walking to work. With male servants at the front line and female staff working for King and country, women who had never had to worry about carrying their front-door key or a sandwich for lunch had to take all they would need for the day in a heroine's handbag.

THE ROARING TWENTIES

When the war ended women were left to contemplate a new set of rules of social etiquette. The huge number of casualties from the war meant that there were fewer eligible men, so unmarried women started to dress up and flirt in order to attract a husband. Hemlines rose, hair was cut and restrictive corsets were thrown away; the new independent woman was

a free spirit and her flapper dress reflected that. Sadly, the differences between the upper and working classes were renewed, with the socialites having a ball and the poor returning to servitude. Most people were not invited to the party that was dubbed the Roaring Twenties. For the women who were, cocktail bags were fancy affairs, elaborately beaded and embroidered. By day the clutch bag, tucked neatly under one arm, flattered the body and kept the smooth lines of the new streamlined silhouette. Travel was fashionable again, and the luxury transatlantic liners became the places to see and be seen. F Scott Fitzgerald was writing *The Great Gatsby* in the USA and Evelyn Waugh was penning *Vile Bodies* in the UK. Motion pictures started being made, Hollywood was created and glamour was everything. The jazz movement enlivened Europe and the USA and the world began to move, literally, to the sound of a new beat. In their new-found freedom, women were also beginning to play sports, especially tennis and golf, and enjoying the new experience of sunbathing on the beach. Many others took to the wheel and learnt to drive. A more active, independent life combined with more wealth meant luggage and handbags could now be luxurious as well as utilitarian.

HERMÈS KELLY

The 1930s was a time of hunger marches in the UK and the Great Depression in the USA. The world slump created an atmosphere that was not conducive to the cocktail party and even the privileged few felt the need to tame their excessive living and expensive habits. Nevertheless, the wealthy still sunbathed in the South of France and Deauville and enjoyed wearing silk pyjamas to bed. The frail economic climate can be illustrated by the fact that Coco Chanel felt it necessary to cut all her prices by half in 1932. Clothes kept the slim silhouette of the 1920s, but the waist returned. Skirts got longer and more sober in style. Handbags remained neat to lie flat against the body and in 1930 Emile Hermès included in his catalogue a 46-cm (18-inch) saddle-style bag for women (it was the original Kelly bag). At this time women were carrying their own lighter and cigarettes (without a holder), following the example set by Wallis Simpson and Coco Chanel. Women were much more independent and flaunted it by wearing

trouser suits. One woman in particular, Amy Johnson, inspired many women by her brave solo flight from the UK to Australia and by the more mannish clothes she chose to wear. Despite the growing independence of women, the prevailing mood towards the end of the decade was one of austerity and anxiety, and the rise of Fascism in Italy and the Nazi movement in Germany brought about another world war in 1939.

NEW LOOK

The doom and gloom of the Second World War was alleviated by a determined effort in every social group to 'make do and mend'. Women of all classes went back to work the land and 'dig for victory', or work in the offices, factories and service industries that were bereft of men. Women could not afford, nor were they allowed, to buy new clothes. Fabric was rationed and London department stores, such as John Lewis, held fittings in basement air-raid shelters so women could try on clothes in safety and avoid the potential embarrassment of being in a state of undress should an alarm be raised. Shoulder bags were introduced at this time as part of the standard military issue.

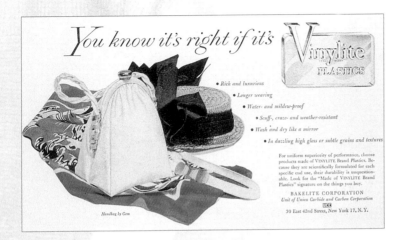

You know it's right if it's **Vinylite** PLASTICS

- Rich and luxurious
- Longer wearing
- Water- and mildew-proof
- Scuff-, craze- and weather-resistant
- Wash and dry like a mirror
- In dazzling high gloss or subtle grains and textures

For uniform superiority of performance, choose products made of VINYLITE Brand Plastics. Because they are scientifically formulated for each specific end use, their durability is unquestionable. Look for the "Made of VINYLITE Brand Plastics" signature on the things you buy.

BAKELITE CORPORATION
Unit of Union Carbide and Carbon Corporation
30 East 42nd Street, New York 17, N. Y.

Handbag by Gem

Even though the zip had been invented by W L Judson in the 1890s, it was only now used as a fastener for bags. The shape of the cardboard gas-mask box everyone carried at all times influenced the bags of the future, with new, more three-dimensional shapes arriving later. For two decades, glamour had been the push behind fashion and accessories, but now necessity and a scarcity of materials dictated fashion and created its own style. Even when the war was over, rationing continued and spirits were understandably low. When, in February 1947, Christian Dior (backed by the textile millionaire, Marcel Boussac) showed his New Look line, which involved 14–75 metres (15–80 yards) of fabric in each outfit, women were overwhelmed by desire. The clothes were everything they could not have. One famous photograph shows a woman dressed in a three-tier swagger coat outside the Dior boutique on Avenue Montaigne, Paris. Noticeably, her bag is big, boxy and crafted from crocodile. The sheer luxury of it all could have provoked another French revolution!

FIFTIES GLAMOUR

Europe was ready, and desperate, to show Hollywood it knew about glamour. Women were enthralled by the apparently perfect lives of the screen goddesses like Veronica Lake, Joan Crawford and later Grace Kelly, Marilyn Monroe and Ingrid Bergman. There was an understandable urge for everything to be 'happy ever after'. When the men came back from war and the economy began to pick up, women returned to the home. Those who were not either extremely rich or working class became housewives. There were new gadgets, like fridges, electric stoves, televisions, vacuum cleaners and cars, available for the growing middle classes. With all the electrical help available, there was no need for servants. For the women who did not marry, there was the opportunity of a career. The idea of a liberated

sexuality was beginning to emerge with the outspoken behaviour of Brigitte Bardot. Her style was quickly copied, like her Vichy gingham wedding dress and her small summery tote bags. The tote was ideal for trips to the beach and shopping sprees, so housewives adopted the bag and took it, along with a smart handbag, when shopping for groceries. Women began to carry one bag for personal belongings and one for shopping because home delivery was on the way out.

Having closed her boutique in Rue Cambon, Paris, in 1939 when war broke out, in 1953 Coco Chanel re-opened her couture business because sales of her scent Chanel No. 5 were dwindling. The first shows had mixed reviews. American *Vogue* adored her modern shapes, but Europe was still in love with the romantic New Look of Dior. When Coco Chanel showed her first quilted bag in 1955, the bag became a timeless classic and the envy of every fashionable woman to date.

THE SWINGING SIXTIES

To the children of the 1950s housewife, the 1960s were an opportunity waiting to happen. Unhampered by the memories of war and rationing, they lived life to the full and were politically fearless in their actions. Nothing could tame the youngster who had grown up in a time of peace, wealth and security. The only threats were the atomic bomb, the Cold War and the repressed behaviour of their parents. The first two problems were dealt with by student protests, which demanded that the government listen to this new generation. The latter problem was countered by the young instigating a sexual revolution, facilitated by the Pill. The thigh-high, knicker-skimming miniskirt just served to state their aims: liberation from home, freedom from the shackles of a monogamous (married) relationship and equality in the workplace. Handbags changed too. Gone were the rigid, conformist shapes favoured by Jackie Kennedy, Princess Grace and the 'prim and proper'. In came the extra-long, hip-length shoulder bags made of fabric or patent leather that looked undeniably shiny and fresh to the eye. The new body shape – gangly, teenage and skinny – suited a new shape of accessory. Hipster

trousers demanded low-slung belts, miniskirts looked great with boots, and skirts got even shorter

with the arrival of tights. Bags, of course, looked better when they were casual and understated, or

absent altogether. After all, no one who was anyone took a handbag to Woodstock.

DISCO FEVER

The 1970s were a decade of differences in fashion. The hip rock-star wedding of Mick and Bianca Jagger showed Bianca in a white trouser suit, but the stately affair of Princess Anne's marriage to Mark Phillips exhibited a high-collared, buttoned-up Susan Small dress, and Princess Caroline wore a floaty white gown when she got married to Phillipe Junot. The idealism of the young people fed on the stability of the wealthy 1960s was to falter and turn into disillusionment and disappointment in the 1970s. The assassinations of John F Kennedy and Martin Luther King in 1963 and 1968 respectively, the student uprisings of 1968 and the Vietnam War were soon to be followed by the political scandal of Watergate and the resignation of President Nixon. Finally, the OPEC oil crisis in 1973 gave rise to an undercurrent of deep unrest. While on the surface disco fever swept through nightclubs, the anarchic feelings that led to punk rock were steadily rising. Young people began to look else-where for inspiration and they were intrigued by other cultures in the pursuit of peaceful living, thus the hippie trail – from Marrakech to India – become the fashionable thing to do. As a result of this exposure to other cultures, ethnic and so-called 'primitive' art became appreciated and was reflected in the fashions of the time. Handbags

were relaxed and informal, preferably picked up on one's travels. The simple two-piece tapestry bag, stitched to a skein of twisted threads to create a shoulder strap, was a popular choice. Meanwhile, Diane Keaton as Woody Allen's Annie Hall (*see opposite*) slung an oversized bag over her shoulder, and disco divas danced around their clutch bags. Diversity was the key word for this decade.

THE POWERHOUSE EIGHTIES

With the arrival of Mrs Thatcher as the UK's first female Prime Minister in 1979, Britain entered the 1980s. After the Winter of Discontent was played out to anarchic punk music, the first steps to a spending boom were taken to

the sounds of New Romantic music. Lady Diana Spencer became a style icon with her pie-crust collars and Laura Ashley skirts, which were soon adopted as the uniform of London's Sloane Ranger. This new group of well-to-do upper middle-class Brits carried shoulder bags by Mulberry or Barbour to retain a look of the

countryside – where, in theory, they owned a country pile –
in the city. Women also succumbed to the Lycra revolution
led by Jane Fonda. Jogging, working out and aerobic classes
meant women began to carry gym bags with them, and

sportswear companies, especially
Reebok and Head, captured the
female market. In the workplace
women were breaking through
the glass ceiling to executive
level – the briefcase became a
mainstay and would, of course,
carry a Filofax. Power dressing
was the order of the day and
luxury labels ruled. Versace
brought sequinned glamour to
the catwalks and Louis Vuitton,
Hermès and Chanel captured
the hearts of all logo collectors.

FULL CIRCLE

Towards the end of the 1990s the information and communication industries had taken hold and many women had a mobile phone and a Psion organizer instead of a Filofax to carry in their Prada rucksacks, as well as a laptop computer to carry in their hands. There was a backlash to the hedonism of the 1980s, brought about by the threat of AIDS and the downturn in the economy. Logos were removed or made discreet, and conspicuous spending, though still existing, was less evident. Minimalist style was just as expensive to achieve as the ostentatious look of a few years earlier. Waif-like models and grunge clothes made fashion come full circle. In the last few years of the 1990s, the fabulously expensive, unravelled and frayed Voyage dresses and cardigans, so adored by

the seriously wealthy, like Jemima Khan and Madonna, have come to epitomize the trend to appear elegantly down at heel – at a price unaffordable to those who really are. Gucci enjoyed a hugely successful revival in the hands of American designer Tom Ford, who began to reintroduce logos back onto the catwalk, and soon it was cool again to have a designer bag. In response, Chanel has created the first ergonomically designed handbag – the 2005 (see *below*) – which is shaped to fit the contours of the body. It is ironic that in the last year of the twentieth century, the fashion pack announced the death of the handbag as we know it. The functional 'body bag' in high-tech, utility fabrics by directional designers such as Helmut Lang (see *right*) and Prada are a welcome change for modern women who are only too happy to let go of prim little handles and embrace the new millennium, hands-free and with open arms.

CHAPTER 2

THE WHO'S
WHO OF HANDBAGS

EVERY ARTIST HAS A MUSE, SOMEONE WHO INSPIRES THEIR CREATIVE IDEAS, A WOMAN WHOSE SENSE OF SELF AND 'ESSENCE' IS POWERFUL ENOUGH TO TRANSLATE INTO AN ART FORM AND BE COMMUNICATED TO THE WHOLE WORLD. THESE CHOSEN FEW CAN BE FILM STARS, ROYALTY, SUPERMODELS OR SIMPLY SOULMATES. WHO HAS NOT DREAMT OF BEING THE INSPIRATION BEHIND A SONG, A BOOK OR A SCENT? THERE IS SOMETHING TERRIBLY ROMANTIC AND IDEALISTIC ABOUT THE WHOLE CONCEPT. HUBERT DE GIVENCHY DESIGNED CLOTHES WITH AUDREY HEPBURN IN MIND, AND CHRISTIAN DIOR CREATED HIS SCENT MISS DIOR FOR HIS SISTER CATERINE, BUT THE ULTIMATE DREAM MUSE HAS TO BE GRACE KELLY. NOT ONLY DID SHE INFLUENCE THE WORK OF FILM DIRECTOR ALFRED HITCHCOCK, SHE WAS ALSO THE INSPIRATION FOR A SCENT – FLEURISSIMO BY CREED. FOR MOST WOMEN, THOUGH, GRACE KELLY WILL BE REMEMBERED FOR THE HANDBAG THAT WAS RE-CHRISTENED IN HER HONOUR. AFTER ALL, FASHIONS MAY DATE AND SCENTS MAY FADE, BUT I HAVE YET TO FIND A WOMAN WHOSE KELLY BAG HAS LOST ITS APPEAL.

F or a bag to achieve cult status it needs to be totally and utterly desirable. Of course, this is determined in part by its design, quality and charm, but a breathtakingly high price tag and a long waiting list make it all the more covetable. However, for a handbag to go down in history as a cult item, it must also be seen on the arms of the world's most fashionable, beautiful and famous women.

HANDBAGS FROM FICTION

For many, the earliest memory of a handbag is Mary Poppins's carpet bag. When P L Travers wrote his children's story about the magical English nanny who arrives on the east wind, he gave her a Gladstone bag from which she pulled all sorts of weird and wonderful things, to the utmost surprise of her charges. If the character had been male, he would have pulled his props from a black top hat in true magician style, but for a woman, a handbag was much more appropriate. The scene in the book also reinforced the idea that women carry everything but the kitchen sink in their handbags.

Another literary handbag that no young school child forgets is the one found in Oscar Wilde's *The Importance of Being Earnest.* When the snobbish

ABOVE: A MULBERRY BAG, REMINISCENT OF MARY POPPINS'S CARPET BAG

Lady Bracknell is checking up on the family connections of Jack Worthing, who wishes to marry her daughter Gwendolen, she is horrified to find he has lost both parents. He explains to her that, in fact, they lost him, and he was found at Victoria Station in a handbag. 'A hand-bag?' she asks. 'Yes Lady Bracknell,' replies Jack. 'I was in a hand-bag – a somewhat large, black leather hand-bag, with handles to it – an ordinary hand-bag in fact.' The scene was immortalized by Edith Evans as Lady Bracknell in Anthony Asquith's elegant adaptation of the play for the cinema in 1952. Evans's incredulous look when she shrieks 'A hand-bag?' is indelibly cast in the minds of all who have seen it.

Small children today are much more likely to be familiar with the handbag collection of Tinky Winky, one of the cuddly characters in the hugely successful TV programme, 'Teletubbies'. When the show was launched in France, Tinky Winky's handbag-carrying caused much consternation among parents who were worried that this feminine behaviour might influence their own offspring and encourage homosexual tendencies.

ABOVE: 'IS THIS THE HANDBAG, MISS PRISM? EXAMINE IT CAREFULLY BEFORE YOU SPEAK.' MICHAEL REDGRAVE AND MARGARET RUTHERFORD IN THE IMPORTANCE OF BEING EARNEST

THE FASHION INTELLIGENTSIA

During the 1950s, Diana Vreeland, editor-in-chief of American *Vogue* and contemporary of Wallis Simpson, announced to her bemused magazine staff, 'We are going to eliminate all handbags'. The adoption of male-style clothing, with all its practical pockets, would make it easier for women to leave their handbags at home, but what Vreeland had not considered was the fact that women actually liked to carry bags. It was *Vogue* that wrote about the 'multiplicity of pockets' on Coco Chanel's suits, with 'real pockets made to hold a key, a lighter, whatever', but when Coco Chanel created her quilted bag with gilt chain straps in 1955, Diana Vreeland was among the first to snap one up.

For hairstylist Frederick Fekkai, whose salon is on the fourth floor of the Chanel building in New York, handbags have become an obsession. He was constantly amazed at the variety of handbags carried by his clients, who included some of the fashion

LEFT: COCO CHANEL
ABOVE: DIANA VREELAND WITH THE ONE-SEAM COAT BY BALENCIAGA

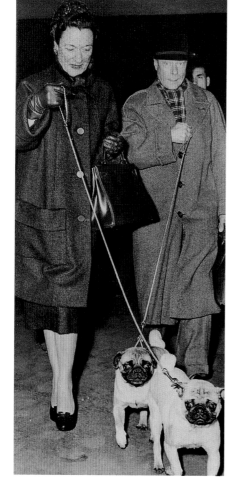

LEFT: THE DUKE AND DUCHESS OF WINDSOR STEP OUT. NOTICE THE INSIGNIA (*RIGHT*) ON HER CROCODILE BAG — TWO WS, FOR WINDSOR AND WALLIS, ENTWINED BENEATH A CROWN

world's most influential and stylish women. After months of seeing what styles worked and what did not, he decided to create his own range that placed function as high as form on the design agenda.

Kate Spade, who was accessories editor on American *Mademoiselle* magazine, had similar reasons for launching her own completely new range of handbags. Like Frederick Fekkai, her position made her privy to insider information that made her acutely aware of what women wanted from their handbags, so she set out to provide it for them. The success of her rapidly growing company shows that she got it right and has managed to fulfil the criteria.

REGAL MUSES

Although public figures naturally have the attention of the world at large, there are only a handful that carry it well, with refinement and respectability. Grace Kelly was one who inspired women with her timeless, pared-down elegance. In 1956 she made the front cover of *Life* magazine in a photograph showing her holding her Hermès *petit sac haut*

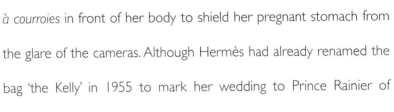

à courroies in front of her body to shield her pregnant stomach from the glare of the cameras. Although Hermès had already renamed the bag 'the Kelly' in 1955 to mark her wedding to Prince Rainier of Monaco, because Grace had carried one throughout most of her engagement, nothing quite prepared them for the effect this cover picture was to have, and there has been a six months' waiting list for a Kelly bag ever since. Not surprisingly, Princess Caroline of Monaco, their first daughter, has become a style icon in her own right and still carries the Kelly bag so favoured by her mother.

Jackie Kennedy, along with her husband, was famously acknowledged as 'American royalty' and she conveyed a sense of perfect decorum and chic style

LEFT: JACKIE KENNEDY IN LONDON
OPPOSITE: GRACE KELLY ARRIVES AT HER PARENTS' HOME FOLLOWING HER ENGAGEMENT
TO PRINCE RAINIER   *ABOVE RIGHT:* THEIR FIRST DAUGHTER, CAROLINE

that was admired worldwide. Every handbag, suit and dress she wore was copied for the crowds of American women infatuated by their First Lady's sense of style and the casual effortlessness with which she carried off even the most 'dressy' outfits. Throughout her life she was photographed by the paparazzi, so her vast collection of handbags have been well documented, and women have been able to imitate her style easily, if not always successfully.

The most beloved member of royalty in recent years, and the one whose impact on fashion may even exceed that of Grace or Jackie, was of course Diana, Princess of Wales. The Lady Dior handbag, with its gold letter charms spelling out D. I. O. R. dangling from the handle, would always have been a best-seller, no doubt, but when Diana started to carry one, the rest of the world's well-dressed – and well-highlighted – women wanted one too. It is a bag that will be long remembered.

RIGHT: THE LADY DIOR HANDBAG WITH ITS GOLD LETTER CHARMS SPELLING OUT D. I. O. R., WORN BY PRINCESS DIANA

THE ACTRESS AND THE HANDBAG

Many column inches in women's magazines have been devoted to actresses and their choice of handbags, though few famous women have had a direct influence on the design of a bag. In 1984 the actress and model Jane Birkin found herself sitting next to Hermès's President Jean-Louis Dumas aboard an airline flight. He saw she was struggling with a large straw tote bag, filled with all the paraphernalia she needed to carry for her small daughter Charlotte. While they travelled, they started to design a bag that would be easy to open and capacious enough to hold everything a young mother might need. The Birkin bag — and another cult must-have — was born.

Catherine Deneuve, the French ex-Chanel model and actress, also shares the honour of having her

LEFT TO RIGHT: **ACTRESS JANE BIRKIN; THE BIRKIN BAG BY HERMÈS; ACTRESS CATHERINE DENEUVE**

LEFT: ACTRESS ALEX KINGSTON AT THE LONDON PREMIERE OF *PRIMARY COLOURS*
BELOW: SHARON STONE

ABOVE LEFT: GERRI 'GINGER SPICE' HALLIWELL
ABOVE: MEG MATTHEWS AND NOEL GALLAGHER

FAR LEFT: MODEL TYRA BANKS AT THE OSCARS, 1996
LEFT: ACTRESS LAURA DERN
RIGHT: PATSY KENSIT
FAR RIGHT: JADE JAGGER AT THE ELLE STYLE AWARDS, 1998

LEFT: MODEL
CLAUDIA SCHIFFER
BELOW: ACTRESS
CATHERINE ZETA JONES

ABOVE: SOCIALITE TAMARA BECKWITH
FAR LEFT: ACTRESS CAMERON DIAZ
LEFT: PRESENTER OPRAH WINFREY

ABOVE: BRITT EKLAND
LEFT: MODEL
KAREN MULDER AT
A VERSACE PARTY

name given to a handbag. The Catherine Deneuve bag by Fendi was designed so Catherine could keep her purse and make-up in the top part, while a secret bottom case held documents or jewellery safely locked away. Deneuve obviously has a passion for handbags because her name crops up on more company client lists than any other (hotly followed by Madonna's).

The recent trend for fashion magazines to forgo models on their covers in favour of celebrities shows just how much actresses and singers can influence our purchases. When American *Vogue* knows it can sell more copies with a picture of Hillary Clinton or Oprah Winfrey on the cover rather than Shalom Harlow or Amber Valetta, you can be sure that a picture of Gwyneth Paltrow or Cameron Diaz carrying a particular handbag or wearing a particular dress will have a similar effect on the sale of those items.

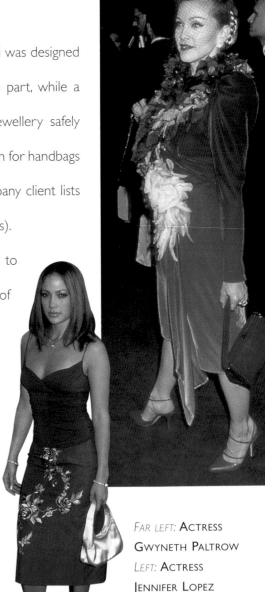

FAR LEFT: ACTRESS GWYNETH PALTROW
LEFT: ACTRESS JENNIFER LOPEZ
ABOVE: MADONNA

STYLE SHAPERS AND SUPERMODELS

Although some companies refuse to say who their famous customers are, there can be no denying the fact that they reap the benefits when newspapers and magazines show pictures of their clients carrying their handbags. The interest generated from the picture of Elizabeth Hurley carrying a sparkling Judith Leiber handbag to the wedding of her friend Henry Dent-Brocklehurst and the model Lili Maltese is far greater than any amount of carefully placed advertising.

The clothes and bags female celebrities choose to wear make a huge impact on fashion for ordinary women. In the 1980s, not one film premiere nor one fashion show was attended without a slew of Chanel bags being seen and photographed, but by the end of the decade Prada bags had replaced Chanel ones at all the

LEFT: ACTRESS CAMERON DIAZ   *ABOVE:* ELIZABETH HURLEY
RIGHT: MADONNA

places to see and be seen. For some, the Lady Dior was the bag of the moment, or the updated Gucci bag with bamboo handles, but both were followed by the Fendi Baguette.

Many style-setters decided to forgo labels altogether by the 1990s, in favour of idiosyncratic styles like antique or delicate beaded

bags found in flea markets and second-hand shops. Helena Christensen and Kate Moss are perfect exponents of this eclectic style. The small, pretty and preferably vintage handbag, which had previously been used only for evening, is now *de rigueur* and works well with the current fashion for floaty slip dresses and tiny cardigans. One look at photographs from the Oscar ceremonies or Royal Ascot clearly shows that, for the moment, handbags are getting smaller and smaller. Perhaps, one day soon, Diana Vreeland's dictum heralding the end of handbags will come true.

OPPOSITE: MODELS ELLE MACPHERSON, JODIE KIDD AND ALEK WEK
ABOVE: MODELS KATE MOSS AND SHALOM HARLOW
RIGHT: MODEL HELENA CHRISTENSEN

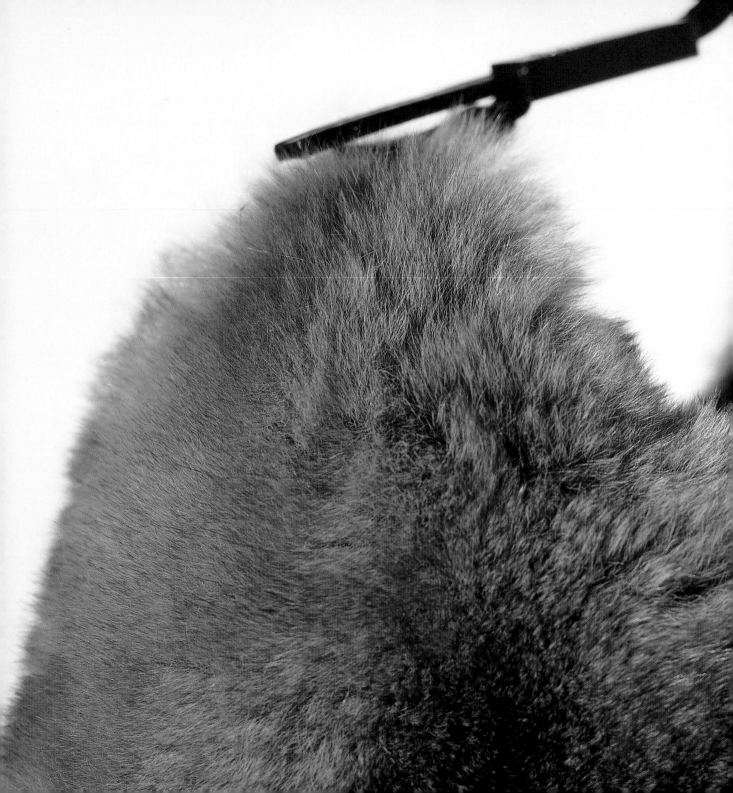

CHAPTER 3

BAGS OF STYLE

THE FREUDIANS WERE THE FIRST TO SEE HANDBAGS AS A SEXUAL INDICATOR, FOLLOWING ON FROM THE EARLY SEVENTEENTH-CENTURY USE OF THE WORD 'PURSE' TO INDICATE FEMALE PUDENDA. CERTAINLY NO WOMAN WANTS TO BE CALLED AN OLD BAG, BUT REVERSE CHIC WOULD ENCOURAGE THE YOUNG AND HIP TO SCOUR FLEA MARKETS FOR EXACTLY THAT ITEM. SO WHAT DOES YOUR CHOICE OF BAG SAY ABOUT YOUR PERSONALITY? ARE YOU AUTHORITATIVE? A STURDY, SAFE HANDBAG. ARE YOU VERSATILE AND SPONTANEOUS? A BACKPACK. ARE YOU OPEN AND ACCESSIBLE? A TOTE BAG. ARE YOU STATUS-CONSCIOUS? A DESIGNER BAG. ALL WILL BE REVEALED . . .

W hat does your choice of handbag say about you? Do the items you carry within it consolidate your outer image? We are all quick to presume the contents of a bag by its outward appearance, and quite often we feel able to judge the character of the person who is carrying it, too.

A SYMBOL OF POWER

The press attention given to the handbag of the ex-Prime Minister Mrs Thatcher (*see left*) is an excellent example. 'That shiny black handbag is as lethal as ever,' ran the *Sun* newspaper. In *The Times*, June 1982, Julian Critchley wrote: 'She has been beastly to the Bank of England, has demanded that the BBC "set its house in order" and tends to believe the worst of the Foreign and Commonwealth Office. She cannot see an institution without hitting it with her handbag.' 'It represented female power – an assertive woman's determination to impose her will on men,' shrieked the *Mail on Sunday*. In time, 'handbagging' became a byword for the way Thatcher dealt with her political opponents. Her sturdy, smart handbags, almost identical to those used by the Queen, became a potent symbol of her authority, in the same way as Winston Churchill's cigar became his. In fact, Churchill College in Cambridge, created to house his papers, has also been chosen by Lady Thatcher to house her letters and speeches, along with some of her famous handbags. In an office environment, the style of bag a person carries can be indicative of their position in the hierarchy. A cinematic example of this is powerfully conveyed by Melanie Griffith in *Working Girl*.

As a secretary her squashy shoulder bag is bulging with clutter, but when she starts carrying Sigourney Weaver's small, streamlined handbags and briefcase Griffith also assumes her boss's business acumen.

SEX AND STATUS

For some, caring about one's appearance often leads to conformity, with all the women in a particular social group dressing in similar attire and choosing the same designers. After all, they belong to an elite 'club'. Gilt-strapped society ladies, with their fabulously expensive and logo-embossed bags, are giving much away about their personalities: they wish to make a show of wealth and status.

Handbags can also convey sex and availability, as in the case of overly made-up single girls wearing short skirts and low-cut tops on a night out, who prefer to dance around their handbags rather than carry them. If their purses do represent the female pudenda, then dancing around them in a disco for all to see is tantamount to a mating call.

Observe the handbags of others, and the choices you make yourself. Your handbag announces your arrival and implies a code of conduct. If you have always been a one-handbag woman, you might decide that now is an opportunity to use different bags according to the time of day, place and occasion.

CLUTCH The clutch is usually for the evening because it is designed to be slim and held in the hand like a document wallet, or tucked neatly under one's arm while holding a glass or being introduced. Discretion is a characteristic of someone choosing this envelope-style bag.

DUFFEL BAG The drawstring top on this bag makes throwing items in and pulling them out easy. Originally a sports bag, the duffel often retains the round or oval base that accommodated a ball.

SHOULDER AND CARTRIDGE BAGS

The long strap allows the shoulders to carry the weight of the bag leaving the hands free to access the contents, making shoulder bags the choice of bus conductors, gamekeepers and postal workers. In fashion terms, the strap is usually slipped over one shoulder so the bag can be shrugged on and off, rather than worn across the body, which distributes the weight more evenly.

HEIRLOOM BAGS Unusual bags are collectors' items and show an eclectic, individual style. Jewellery designer Angela Hale collects bags from every era, from beaded evening bags to ones made from Bakelite. Acquire one of your own by hunting through your attic for grandma's old handbags.

EVENING BAGS Smaller and more decorative than day bags, these are the bags that give a little more of one's character away. A simple black velvet clutch shows a formal, restrained attitude, while a sparkling, colourful minaudière expresses a more exuberant personality.

KELLY BAG Women do not carry a Kelly bag (whether the real thing from Hermès, or one of the many fake imitations) unless they like what it stands for – namely the beauty, wealth, talent and style of Princess Grace.

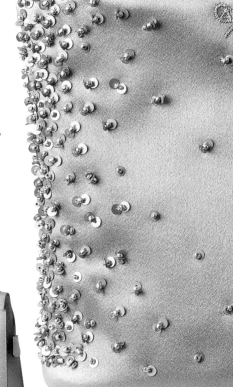

VANITY CASE The woman who has a specially constructed bag for her stash of creams, lotions and potions is not necessarily vain, but she certainly cares about her appearance.

LOGO-EMBOSSED DESIGNER BAG The owner of this bag aspires to the lifestyle that that particular designer reflects. Do you wish to indulge in a little of the rock-star glamour a Versace bag might bring, or do you prefer a dose of Gallic chic from Chanel?

EMBROIDERED BAGS Loved by those who are arty and prefer quirkiness to uniformity, the delicate embroidered bag is not for those who want a standardized product.

PURSE The bag within a bag, the purse holds money and other precious possessions, such as photographs and documents. A bulging purse shows a busy person who likes to cling on to things, whereas the slim, smart purse reveals a more ordered life and mind.

THE BUCKET BAG (CABOT) A casually chic multi-tasker, this classic wide-topped bag easily holds a great number of items within its roomy confines. Functional and stylish, the nylon Hervé Chapelier cabot, in particular, became an early 1990s 'must-have' when fashion and practicality merged.

MINAUDIÈRE This is the bag as a work of art, and is not for the faint-hearted. 'Look at me,' it shouts. The rhinestone-encrusted evening bags by Judith Leiber stand out and demand attention. The word *minaudière* apparently means 'coquettish air', and was coined by Alfred Van Cleef, the jeweller, when he saw Florence Gould, the wife of an American railroad magnate, use a metal cigarette box as a small handbag.

BACKPACK Like the shoulder bag, a backpack allows the weight of the contents to be carried evenly by the body, which is why European children always wear their satchels over both shoulders. In contrast, the traditional British school satchel weighs heavily on one shoulder and is often the reason behind slouches and bad deportment. During the late 1980s and the 1990s, Miuccia Prada took the backpack from the

playground to the front rows of the fashion shows, ensuring that the convenient (and accommodating) rucksack became stylish.

THE TOTE A tote is the perfect grocery or beach bag. The open top reveals an open personality; the contents are easily seen and there is nothing to conceal. Although versions range from the utterly practical to the more stylized, one of the best examples is made by the American company L L Bean. Originally designed to carry ice down from the mountains, the canvas is still treated to make it resistant to mildew.

THE SOCIALITE

Daphne still thinks that people who come out are débutantes. Her life is her social diary, but she likes to call it her charity work. Her motto is 'give glamorously', and in doing so she fits in an awful lot of organizational lunches. Every maître d' in town knows her and her small coterie of friends. The contents of her handbag are a testament to her lifestyle, which begins with a little shopping in the morning (on account, of course, and delivered to her home) and a fortifying cup of coffee at her members-only club, where she can read all the gossip columns in peace and quiet. Over lunch she never forgets to take a selenium tablet because simply everyone has told her the supplement keeps old age and sagging skin at bay. In the event of a face-lift, her hairdresser and colourist has promised to tell her which doctor gets the best results — after all, she gets to see all the scars behind the hairline. In the meantime, the 'lady who lunches' gets by with a little designer make-up — she does not like all that trendy matt black packaging, but prefers gilt. Sometimes she will hang on to opera tickets and race meeting cards as mementoes of great parties.

THE CAREER WOMAN

Time is of the essence for the career woman. To fit in with her busy workload, her briefcase has to be streamlined and functional. She has a checklist for the contents of each bag, which she ticks off meticulously: passport, frequent flyer card, phone cards for each country, mobile phone, Psion organizer, and currency for tipping. She collects hotel repair kits, so she is never caught with a loose button or hem, and she hangs on to foreign receipts – especially Prada and Gucci – just so she can check how much she saved when she gets home. Hand cream, for a firm but smooth handshake, is her concession to femininity in the boardroom, and strong mints are really for offering to less sweet-smelling business clients. She loves Trish McEvoy's make-up planner and the classic smell of Chanel No. 5. She could not live without her laptop and her Psion, but she still likes to have a Montblanc for signing documents.

THE MODEL

Days spent walking from one office to another on 'go-sees' means the young model keeps all her creature comforts to hand in her rucksack. Alongside the essential bottle of mineral water (invariably still and Evian), there is, more often than not, a packet of Marlboro Lights and matches from the bars visited the night before. Sugar-free chewing gum gets rid of smoky breath and a quick spritz of scent will do the rest. Discount cards for cosmetic stores and a collection of lipsticks and eye-shadows given to the model by make-up artists on shoots also make an appearance. A pair of Calvin Klein sunglasses – the same style Kate Moss wore in the ad – cover up jet-lagged eyes, while reviving aromatherapy sprays combat cabin dehydration. Tarot cards are the model's latest craze, but they sometimes distract her so much that she forgets her Filofax and city maps. She never carries her mobile phone in her bag, since it is always clamped safely against her ear.

THE MOTHER

Since giving birth, the new mother has had a radical life change. Gone is the career bag; she now could

not live without her wipe-clean Kate Spade black nylon tote. Keeping calm is of major concern, so she

bought a chakra-balancing necklace of semi-precious gems, but cannot wear it because the baby pulls

if off. Into the bag goes the necklace, along with a small packet of sweets to pacify the baby, vitamins,

reviving essential oils and *The Little Book of Calm*, although she secretly feels that a slick of lipstick and a

spray of scent does much more for her spirit than any amount of camomile tea. She has become a Friend

of the nearby museum (it makes walking the baby much more interesting), and her only store card now

is for the pharmacy. Seeing all the career girls dashing around town,

the mother looks down at her baby in the pushchair and

does not regret a moment.

THE PARTY GIRL

Life is just one long invitation for the party girl. Late nights and long mornings spent at the hairdresser's mean a party girl needs every little help she can get to prevent her spirits from flagging. Vitamin sachets keep energy her levels soaring and pick-me-up tonics help to kick-start the day and can even be mixed with champagne for a boosting cocktail. Maximum-strength tablets eradicate hangover headaches, but on those 'fragile' days she skips the blow-dry (too noisy) and makes do with jewelled hair slides, a pair of shades and a Nars multiple stick to add colour to a sleep-deprived complexion. A Chanel compact and brush is always on standby to banish a shiny nose brought on by dancing too long. The party girl cannot resist a small silver mobile phone for organizing friends for drinks at one of the bars where she is a member. Her favourite scent at the moment is Flirt (a great name) and her favourite possession is her Return to Tiffany's key ring, given to her by her last squeeze.

CHAPTER **4**

THE **A–Z** OF HANDBAGS

THERE MUST BE AN IMELDA MARCOS OF THE HANDBAG WORLD, A WOMAN WHO HAS BOUGHT ALMOST ALL STYLES AND MAKES OF HANDBAG TO SATISFY HER PASSION FOR HAVING EVERY LABEL, LITERALLY, AT HER FINGERTIPS. HOWEVER, MOST WOMEN SEEM TO BECOME ATTACHED TO A FEW HOUSES AND ADHERE FAITHFULLY TO THEIR DESIGNS. GONE ARE THE DAYS WHEN A WOMAN WOULD HAVE A WARDROBE OF DAY AND EVENING BAGS FROM WHICH TO CHOOSE. BECAUSE FASHION CHANGES SO QUICKLY NOW, EVEN THE MOST SERIOUS SHOPPERS HAVE ADOPTED THE 'BUY, USE, DISCARD' APPROACH. FAKE DESIGNER HANDBAGS SPEED UP THE TURNOVER OF POPULAR DESIGNS – AFTER ALL, WHO WANTS TO HANG ON TO A CERTAIN STYLE WHEN EVERYONE HAS ONE? THE RAPID CHANGES IN FASHION MAKE COMPILING A LIST OF COMPANIES AND DESIGNERS A DIFFICULT TASK. FASHION EDITORS, BUYERS AND CURRENT DESIGNERS WERE ASKED FOR THEIR OPINIONS. ALL THE COMPANIES INCLUDED HAVE A STRONG TRADITION THAT MAKES THEM INSTANTLY RECOGNIZABLE BY WOMEN OF DIFFERENT AGES AND NATIONALITIES.

AIGNER
HORSEPLAY

Discreet, though recognizable by the small inverted horseshoe logo, Aigner handbags have always been popular with European women for their simple, elegant shapes and fine workmanship. Etienne Aigner was born in Hungary at the turn of the century but moved to Paris in the 1930s where he learnt the craft of treating and working with leather. By the 1940s he was confident enough to work alone and designed exclusive bags for small Parisian couture houses like Lanvin and Rochas. In the 1950s he moved to New York and began making leather goods under his own name. The company was officially founded in Munich, Germany, in 1965, and Etienne Aigner's monogram was changed slightly into the horseshoe logo that still remains today. By 1975 Etienne Aigner No. 1, the first designer fragrance for men, was launched, and three years later the first fashion collections for men and women were shown. There are now over 100 Aigner shops in 37 countries.

BILL AMBERG
THE ACCIDENTAL HANDBAG

Although Bill Amberg grew up in Northamptonshire, the home of the English leather trade, he did not plan his career there. In fact, he tried many jobs, including a stint on an oil rig, before moving to Australia in the 1970s where he starting working with a group of leather craftsmen, a liaison which resulted in exhibitions in Sydney, Melbourne and Adelaide. When he returned to the UK in 1982 he set up his own company specializing in leather designs. Amberg has not limited himself to accessories but has been commissioned to do special projects, such as the webbing harness for Tom Cruise in the film *Mission: Impossible*, leather walls, floors and shelves in an Aspen ski chalet, and the reception desk and lift interiors of The Metropolitan hotel in London. With the birth of his second daughter to journalist Susie Forbes, fashion features director of British *Vogue*, he

has designed a leather baby holder. Amberg prides himself on blending the elements of traditional craftsmanship with an insight into the modern-day requirements of bags for work, travel and free time. He also designs ranges for Donna Karan, Margaret Howell, Romeo Gigli and Coach Leather. In 1998 he opened his first store on Ledbury Road in London's trendy Notting Hill district.

B A R B O U R
W A X I N G L Y R I C A L

Barbour are, of course, more well known for their wax jackets than

their handbags, but there was a time in the 1980s when a Barbour cartridge-

style bag became a symbol of the London Sloane Ranger. Made from

thorn-proof canvas, with leather straps and bindings and brass fastenings, the bags

were more often seen in the city than at point-to-points. The cult of the Sloane Ranger

was created by Anne Barr and Peter York from a feature they did for *Harpers & Queen* magazine.

Key to being a Sloane Ranger was living in close proximity to London's Sloane Square but also

having a life in the country at the weekend. A well-used cartridge bag and Barbour jacket for

walking up and down the King's Road in the rain was *de*

rigueur. The fashion spread to Europe and the USA, and

from 1980 to 1989 total sales grew twelvefold.

The company was established in South Shields, England,

in 1894 by John Barbour, a Scottish farmer, who started using oiled

cotton for waterproof clothing, which was made above his small store.

Fishermen were among the first to appreciate the cloth, but word soon

spread and in 1908 the first Barbour catalogue appeared.

C A R T I E R
J E W E L   I N   T H E   C R O W N

In 1901 the Cartier workshops were working at fever pitch to supply 27 diadems that had been ordered from royal courts around the world for the coronation of Edward VII in London. At the time, the future King of England remarked, 'Cartier, jeweller of kings and king of jewellers'. The French company was founded in 1847 but soon became known to a far wider circle than the Parisians because of its unusual designs and fabulous quality. In 1924, for example, Louis Cartier designed the three-band Rolling Ring

in honour of his friend Jean Cocteau; the white gold symbolized friendship, the yellow gold loyalty and the pink gold love. However, it was not until 1974 that Cartier decided to launch the Cartier Leather Collection in its distinctive luminous burgundy colour. In 1990, the Panthère theme (a favourite of Wallis Simpson, who first started to wear a Cartier Panthère brooch in 1948) was used in the

LEFT: HAPPY BIRTHDAY. ESTELLE HALLIDAY AND CLAUDIA CARDINALE CARRY THE CARTIER 150TH ANNIVERSARY BAG

leather collection (*see above*). The feline shape was stylized to decorate the clasps, while the linings were spotted in tribute to the panther's coat. Last year, to celebrate 150 years of Cartier, the Happy Birthday bag (*see opposite, left*) was launched. The burgundy leather, a shade exclusive to Cartier and somewhere between raspberry and wine, was used, with the double C motif embossed in a random pattern like a fireworks display. Jerry Hall, Lisa Marie Presley and Claudia Cardinale each have one.

CELINE

BEST FOOT FORWARD

It is a little-known fact that Celine started in 1946 as a small shop selling children's shoes and boots in the Rue de Malte, Paris. The Children's Bootery, as it was known, was *the* place to go for well-heeled families. By 1958 the Celine family started selling the Inca loafer – a French version of the American penny loafer – adorned with a horse-bit, which quickly became synonymous with Celine leather goods. Five years later the family launched the first shoes for women, followed by the legendary faux-pony print, a design that was picked up again by Michael Kors in his first collection for the house in 1998 (*see opposite, top*). Kors's recent collaboration with Robert Page, head of design for accessories at Celine, marks a turning point for the label. Celine classics have been reinterpreted by using modern fabrics, including neoprene (*see opposite, far right*). The MC 1999 shoulder bag from the Plaque Anneau line is a prime example; 5,000 have been bought every year for the past 30 years and the numbers are increasing.

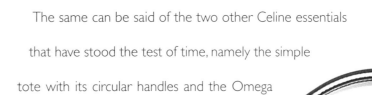

The same can be said of the two other Celine essentials

that have stood the test of time, namely the simple

tote with its circular handles and the Omega

1427 with extendible sides that can be worn

over the shoulder or hand-held.

Although there are now 108 Celine boutiques – including one

in Monte Carlo that was re-opened by Princess Caroline after its

renovation in 1993 – and 502 additional outlets, the company looks

set to expand soon. Kors's new spin on this traditional

French brand, and the excitement that

he will generate, is awaited with

much anticipation. Perhaps he

will work the same magic

Tom Ford did for Gucci – in

which case it is probably

best to put your name

down now for his next

version of the Omega.

CHANEL
THE CHAIN GANG

Of all the 'must-haves' that every modern woman aspires to, a gilt-chained Chanel bag is certainly one. The distinctive chain shoulder strap, threaded with leather, was inspired by Coco Chanel's use of flat-sided chains that were sewn into the hems of

her jackets to help them hang beautifully. Although Coco Chanel started designing in July 1915, when she opened her *maison de couture* in Biarritz, France, she did not design handbags until 1955. In fact, she had closed her atelier in Rue Cambon, Paris, in 1939 with the onset of the Second World War and only re-opened it in 1953 when prompted by the company that sold her perfumes, by which time she was 70 years old.

The first handbags were made in jersey and leather in shades of beige, brown, navy and black. The quilting technique is thought to have been a way of making the

jersey – her signature material – more suitable for the purpose of a handbag, but was also used for leather versions. The linked C logo was not on the original bags (*see below, left*) and was only added in the late 1960s. Since Karl Lagerfeld has been at the helm of Chanel, many inventive and humorous bags have been designed, such as the brightly coloured sheepskin bags of winter 1997 (*see overleaf, top*) and ones with clips to hold newspapers.

Above: **C** OR NOT 2 C – NAOMI CAMPBELL ON THE CATWALK

The latest Chanel bag, the revolutionary 2005 (*see opposite*), has a rigid frame but is shaped to fit the contours of the body and can even be used as a pillow. The bag is available in leather, tweed or jersey.

HERVÉ CHAPELIER
FRENCH REVOLUTION

Chapelier means 'hatter' in French, but that did not stop Hervé Chapelier from deciding to concentrate on another kind of accessory – handbags. Born in 1950 in the fashionable French resort of Biarritz, Hervé grew up surrounded by the stylish people who holidayed there. Although his education in Bordeaux did not involve design and, in fact, he went to business school, an artistic streak runs through the family; one sister is an artist and the other is a florist. At the age of 26, Hervé created a light, useful duffel bag from pieces of nylon, which was an instant hit – not just for being lightweight but also for coming in a huge range of colours. He followed it up with his famous lightweight two-tone trapeze-shaped bag. More recently, his mini-rucksack has enjoyed the same fame. His bags work so well and are loved by many women because they look equally stylish at the gym or the office, with jeans or a suit. The contrasting colourways and sturdy saddle stitching sets them apart from his many imitators. Hervé Chapelier was the first handbag designer to make nylon cool and desirable – something Prada did only 15 years later.

COACH
THE AMERICAN DREAM

In true stars-and-stripes style, the American company Coach started with a baseball glove. When the founder of Coach first discovered the distinctive markings and qualities of the leather that was being used to make baseball gloves – and its incredible suppleness despite hard wear and rough handling – he decided that it would be perfect for handbags. The leather was refined slightly, but left natural to allow the grain to show and burnish beautifully with age. The year was 1941, and at the time the idea was quite revolutionary among the smart American women of the day.

The business was originally a family-run affair of six artisans, who operated from a Manhattan loft. Although the company is still based in midtown Manhattan, the workforce has increased to the hundreds, and the leather artisans are still considered among the best in the USA. The company's philosophy has remained steadfastly the same: their bags must have the unique, clean Coach look that is immediately identifiable. They must be

handmade using organic leather that is completely 'naked', so it burnishes easily and takes on the rich patina of a well-worn saddle.

Coach is to handbags what Levi's is to jeans – an American classic.

84

CONNOLLY
A DRIVING FORCE

If you have ever been driven in a Rolls Royce, Aston Martin, Ferrari or Morgan, or if you regularly travel on Concorde, then you have already come into contact with Connolly. This exclusive British company has been upholstering coaches and cars since 1878 when two brothers, Samuel and Joseph Connolly, opened for business. Soon after, they were commissioned by the Palace to make leather seats for Edward VII's Coronation Coach. After 117 years of supplying the finest leather to prestige marques as well as to private customers, Connolly decided to broaden their horizons and enter the world of luxury leather goods. In 1995 the Connolly shop – designed by Andrée Putman – was opened in the old Belgravia Stables in London. Although a range of handbags for women has not yet been designed as such, the sleek

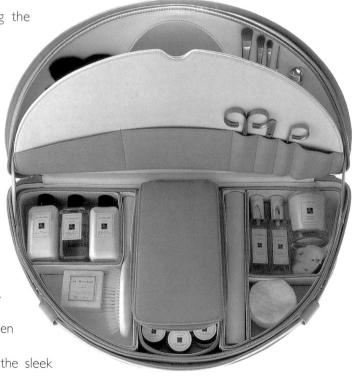

Connolly City rucksack

(*see below right*) is worn

and recognized by women

in the know – usually those

who grew up being driven to

school every day in the Roller.

DIOR
A CHRISTIAN FOLLOWING

Christian Dior was 41 in 1946 when he opened the couture house at 30, Avenue Montaigne, Paris, under his own name. His first collection the following year was dubbed the New Look by Carmel Snow, the influential editor of *Harper's Bazaar,* and since

then the house of Dior quickly moved into other areas of design and accessories, including perfumery, jewellery, tableware, cosmetics and babywear.

In 1957, Yves St Laurent replaced Christian Dior, who had been struck down by a sudden heart attack. Subsequent designers for Dior have been Marc Bohan, Gianfranco Ferre and, since 1997, John Galliano. Galliano has injected freshness while continuing to keep the unashamedly feminine feel and look that is so very Dior and which can be seen clearly in the handbags.

In 1996, Dior sponsored the Cezanne exhibition at the National Galleries of the Grand Palais, which was inaugurated by a gala dinner attended by the late Diana, Princess of Wales. That evening she carried the best-selling classic Dior bag (see *above*), which is available in three sizes, 20 types of material and 53 colours. The four fobs spelling D. I. O. R. hang from the handle and make the handbag instantly recognizable. After that night the bag was renamed the Lady Dior as a tribute to Diana.

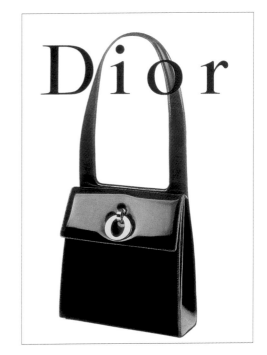

F E N D I
T H E R O M A N E M P I R E

Fendi's fame and fortune goes back to small beginnings. In 1925, two brothers, Edoardo and Adele Fendi, began making fur coats and small leather goods from their workshop in Via del Plebiscito in Rome, but it was not until 1946 that they opened a shop. Their five sisters, Anna, Paola, Franca, Carla and Alda, then joined the business and became the driving force behind the company's success. Their first stroke of genius was to take Karl Lagerfeld on board to design the furs in 1965. He played down the heavy, old-style, status-symbol look of traditional fur coats and used inlaying, varnishing and interweaving to give the coats a fresh, young, fashionable feel. The leather goods underwent a similar transformation, and when the president of Bloomingdale's saw the accessories while in Rome, he decided to take Fendi to the USA.

The double F logo became an instant hit and Fendi took off internationally. In the 1970s the company developed a special etched leather they called *granapaglia*, which was very supple, durable and instantly recognizable. Their best-selling items are the Catherine Deneuve bag, which was specially created

for the actress, and more recently the Baguette (see *opposite*), which has become the bag adored by the fashion pack. Called the Baguette because the shorter shoulder strap means it sits under the arm like a loaf of French bread, the bag is made in a variety of materials from woven raffia to cow-print pony hair – one version for every day of the week. In its 70-plus years of business Fendi has been patronized by women as diverse as Audrey Hepburn, Jackie Kennedy Onassis, Princess Margaret, Madonna and Yoko Ono. Hot on the heels – or rather from the oven – of the Baguette bag comes the Fendi Croissant bag (see *above right*). This mini version of the Baguette still tucks away neatly under one's arm, but is smaller and curved.

SALVATORE FERRAGAMO

SHOEMAKER TO THE STARS

It is impossible to talk about Salvatore Ferragamo without talking about shoes. Although there are now fashion shows, fragrances and shops, Ferragamo will always be inextricably linked to footwear, and handbags and small leather goods were a natural progression. Salvatore Ferragamo was born to a poor family in 1898 in the small village of Bonito, near Naples, Italy. He wanted to become a shoemaker and made his first pair for his sister's Holy Communion when he was just nine years old. In 1914 he joined his three brothers in Santa Barbara, California, where they opened a shoe-repair shop. The burgeoning movie studios in the area became the source of much of their work and Salvatore soon had Mary Pickford and Rudolph Valentino among his clients. He returned to Italy in 1936, settling in Florence and exporting to the USA.

During the Second World War and the Fascist period, heavy restrictions were placed on raw materials. As a result, Ferragamo quickly started to experiment with unusual mediums, such as cork, which he used to create the first wedge shoes, and nylon fishing line, with which he fashioned his famous 'invisible' shoe. This innovative style extends to the handbags, which in recent years have made use of such unexpected materials as Perspex and aluminium. He died prematurely in 1960, leaving his wife Wanda and their children to continue and expand the business. There are now 38 shops and many more outlets worldwide. Ferragamo shoes and handbags are synonymous with 'made in Italy' style and quality.

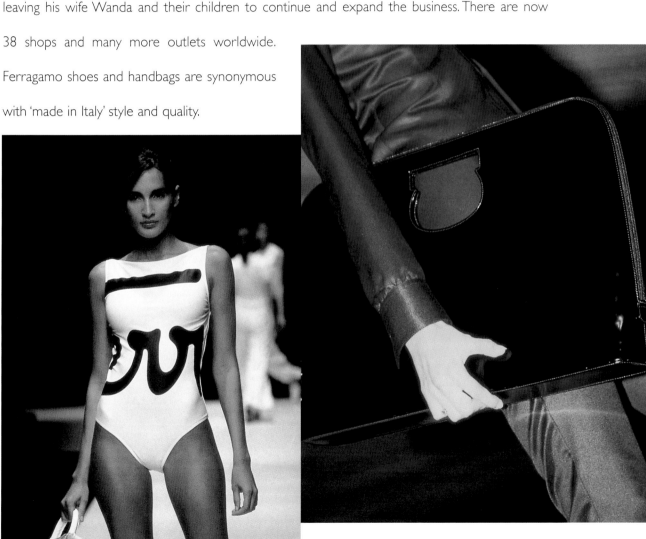

GUCCI

HITTING THE G SPOT

The first thing you notice is the snaffle. It is there on the belts, the loafers and the handbags. Gucci originally traded as saddlers and is proud of its horsey, well-heeled roots. That is not to say the company has always enjoyed the cult status of today. In 1990 Dawn Mello was brought in from the New York store Bergdorf Goodman to revamp a label that had fallen into the luxury trap. Everybody who wanted a Gucci handbag had one because fakes were rife. After eliminating 10,000 of the more dubiously designed products, Mello appointed Tom Ford, the American designer known for his pared-down, stylishly sexy clothes. Ford's first show in 1995 went down as a 'fashion moment' – the models, the clothes and, most importantly, the handbags were to die for.

A Gucci bag was once again as covetable as it had been in the 1950s when Audrey Hepburn, Grace Kelly and Brigitte Bardot carried them.

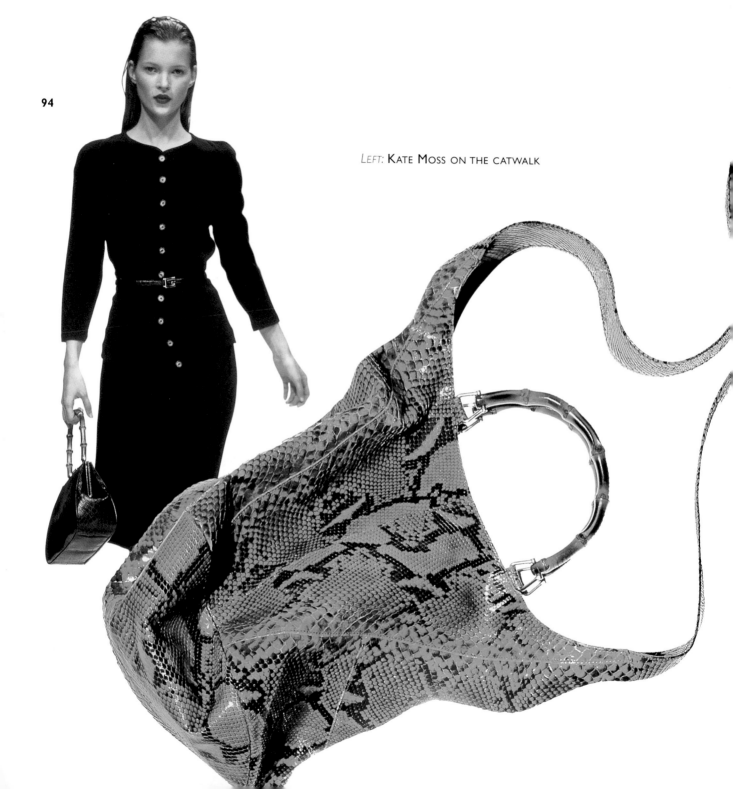

LEFT: KATE MOSS ON THE CATWALK

Although Tom Ford has used the traditional bamboo handles and snaffle decoration, he has cleverly updated them for the new customer without alienating the old (see *this page and opposite*). Bamboo is paired with slinky python or afghan fur, while the snaffle has been stylized into more abstract forms that transport it from the tack box to something more sculptural and sexy. Once again the logo has reached the iconic status it enjoyed in the 1950s and 1980s, and looks set to remain that way for a long time to come.

L U L U   G U I N N E S S
L I F E ' S   A   B A G   O F   R O S E S

When Lulu Guinness left her job in a video production company in 1989, she could not possibly have hoped for the success she has enjoyed in the ten years that followed. From the basement of her house in West London she began creating whimsical handbags that have become works of art. Two of her signature floral handbags, the Florist Basket (see *right*) and the Violet Hanging Basket, became part of the permanent fashion collection at the Victoria & Albert Museum in London. In 1995 she opened a shop with the fashion designer Selina Blow in Elizabeth Street in Pimlico, London, and a year later her own beautiful salon was opened in Ledbury Road, in the fashionable area of Notting Hill, where Bill Amberg (see *page 69*) has his shop. Her client list includes Madonna, Christian Lacroix, Elizabeth Hurley and Dame Judi Dench, for whom she designed the elegant clutch bag that was worn to the 1997 Academy Awards.

Lulu Guinness loves old-style glamour and this is reflected in her handbags, which make heavy use of unusual trims, beading and embroidery. She employs a team of ladies living in the English countryside who hand-embroider her bags, the eldest of whom is 85. Each bag contains a rose-petal card with the name of the lady who embroidered it and the bags have quickly become collectors' items. The emphasis she places on old-fashioned excellence is carried through to the service in her shops. Every customer who has ever bought a bag receives a card that entitles them to use the ladies' room, drop off heavy bags, shelter from the rain or have a cup of tea in the shop. Lulu Guinness offers her customers the same kind of care and attention to detail that have made her delicately feminine bags so successful the whole world over.

NATHALIE HAMBRO
ARTS AND CRAFTS

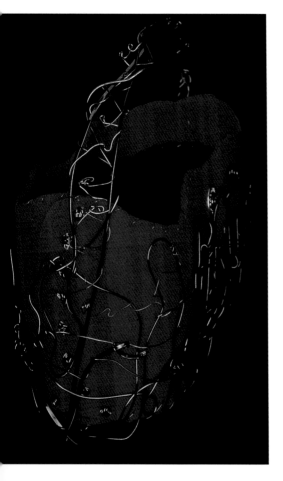

You would be forgiven for not knowing who Nathalie Hambro is, or where her bags are sold; few of her pieces get passed the auction houses and museums that exhibit them. In London, both Sotheby's and the Victoria & Albert Museum show her work. Designed, made and finished by her own hand, Hambro creates unusual, sculptural bags that defy fashion and make light of practicality. Some of her designs, such as the bronze mesh Cabat bag, are too fragile to use, while her Japanese Inro bags are simply too beautiful to put to practical use.

All of her pieces are memorable works of art, and for this reason she designs handbags and jewellery for the couture house of Balmain. Although Hambro is French-born, she has lived in England for the past 26 years and has adopted British nationality. One of her first designs was an aluminium lunchbox, based on traditional Indian tiffin boxes. It became a cult item and is just one of many examples of how Nathalie takes the ordinary and transforms it into something extraordinary.

SAMANTHA HESKIA

BAUBLES, BANGLES AND BEADS

Beadwork has become a byword for Samantha Heskia's covetable handbags. A relative newcomer on the scene, her bags were soon snapped up by fashion editors and those in the know. Unfortunately for Heskia, that meant her bags have been copied mercilessly for high-street chains, but as imitation is the most sincere form of flattery, her name has become extremely well known in a relatively short period of time. Born in London, Heskia is the daughter of a Persian antique textile dealer, so she became interested in art from an early age. After studying in the UK at Chelsea Arts School and in the USA at the Rhode Island School of Design, she worked for an interior design firm, where one of her first commissions was to design the inside of a Boeing 747. She then moved on to the film industry, and while working on film sets she created her first beaded bag collection. Her handbags were quickly bought by designers, actresses and models, such as Edina Ronay, Kate Capshaw, Helena Christensen and Yasmin Le Bon.

HERMÈS
RIDING HIGH

The approach they adopt at Hermès is that shaking up tradition is the only way to respect it. The company began in 1837 when Thierry Hermès opened a workshop for horse and harness equipment after training at Pont Audemer, the main centre for leather work in France. His second son, Charles Emile, assisted him, and won a prize for design at the Paris World Fair in 1878, which helped him to open a saddlery at the prestigious address 24, Rue Fauberg Saint-Honoré. Hermès soon began to supply the courts of Europe, and the tradition for excellence and working for royalty began. However, it was Grace Kelly in the 1950s who gave Hermès the worldwide recognition it has now. During her engagement to Prince Rainier of Monaco, she was photographed many times with her favourite Hermès bag, which the company renamed 'the Kelly' (*see above right*) when they wed. That particular style of bag was originally designed in 1892 as a 'roomy, trapezoidal leather bag with a clasp, intended to hold a rider's saddle and boots', but in 1930

Emile Hermès made a smaller 46-cm (18-inch) version for women, which became the 'ladies'
travel bag with strap'. Other bags, such as the Bugatti and the Birkin (*see overleaf, top left*), have
become equally covetable, but would-be-owners have to be prepared for a waiting list
of at least three months.

In 1997 the Belgian-born designer Martin Margiela was appointed designer for the ready-to-wear business, but the accessory side continues to make news. The latest collaboration has been with the Yawanawas tribe of Brazilian Indians, and Hermès has begun to work with a new substance called Amazonia, a plant-based material made from hevea sap and applied to cotton cloth. The sap is collected between April and November when the trees are pierced in the hours before sunrise. Amazonia shares many of the same qualities as leather – it is a natural, living material and does not tear. Hermès has used the material to great acclaim in the Herbag design (*see opposite*).

RIGHT: MODEL ELLE MACPHERSON

ANYA HINDMARCH

BUY IT WITH A BOW

Anya Hindmarch's first love began at 14 – it was with an old Gucci handbag given to her by her mother. At 17 she went to Florence to learn Italian and returned with a leather drawstring bag that she had noticed all the Florentine women carrying. A year later, Anya Hindmarch was designing and selling her first collection of handbags. The first stroke of luck – or first sign of success to come – was when she designed a bag for a reader's offer in British *Harpers & Queen*, which generated 500 orders. Hindmarch is quintessentially English and there is always something quirky about her designs – she has injected humour into the handbag and that is what makes her different. Her trademark little bow is now recognized by the same Florentine women she once set out to emulate.

D O N N A K A R A N
T A K I N G I T E A S Y

It is easy to see why fashion designer Donna Karan is called 'the Queen of New York'. Women look up to her, and her designs, because she knows what women want – simple pieces, like stretch-jersey bodies and wrap-around skirts that make them look slimmer and can be worn with the minimum of fuss.

Fashion design and clothes are a part of Donna's lifeblood. Her stepfather was in the Seventh Avenue rag trade, her father was a tailor and her mother, Helen 'Richie' Faske, was a model. Donna worked for Anne Klein, then set up her own business in 1985 with her sculptor husband Stephan Weiss. Her aim was to create a 'compromise between tailoring and sportswear', and her diffusion range DKNY serves the sportswear aspect while the Donna Karan label provides the tailoring approach. Her handbags also meet this brief. Whatever the fabric or design, a Donna Karan handbag will always serve its purpose while looking smart and stylish.

ORLA KIELY
IRISH CHARM

Emerging now as one of the most innovative accessories designers around, Orla Kiely makes great use of vibrant colours and unusual materials and shapes to create handbags that are both practical and fresh in design. With her handbags garnering a great deal of press attention, the Kiely label is poised to expand.

Raised in Dublin, Ireland, Orla Kiely first showed artistic promise at the local convent school that she attended. After studying at the Royal College of Art, where she gained a masters degree in textiles, Orla then went on to work for such blue-chip companies as Habitat, Marks & Spencer and Esprit before starting up her own label. Still relatively small, this is one label to watch.

CALVIN KLEIN

MASTER OF THE MINIMAL

Calvin Klein knows how to create a scandal. In the 1970s he did it with an advertisement for his jeans showing Brooke Shields and the words, 'Nothing comes between me and my Calvins'. In the 1990s he did it once again with the startling black-and-white photographs for his unisex scent cKone, showing Kate Moss and anti-fashion, anti-hero types huddled in groups, united only by the whiff of the cologne.

Despite the raunchy image presented by his advertising campaigns, the words invariably used to describe his clothes are 'minimal', 'pared-down' and 'beautifully cut'. Calvin Klein's emphasis on simple cut and comfortable materials have made both his clothing and underwear lines immensely wearable and popular.

His CK diffusion range has shoes and handbags that closely follow the vagaries of fashion, but are tempered to fit the casual simplicity of the line by the use of hardwearing materials in just a few colours.

LAUNER
HOLDING THE ROYAL PURSE STRINGS

Whether the Queen is on official business in India, spending a day at Ascot or attending the State Opening of Parliament, the sturdy, practical handbags fitting neatly over her arm are always Launer. Needless to say, the company prefers longevity and luxury rather than fleeting fashions and eye-catching trends. Form, function and quality are the tenets of Gerald Bodmer's company, founded just over 50 years ago. Surprisingly, Bodmer started his career as a musician, studying the clarinet at the Royal College of Music in London and

LEFT: A SOLDIER LOOKS AFTER HER MAJESTY'S HANDBAG AT THE TROOPING OF THE COLOUR

working with the Carla Rosa Opera Company and the BBC. When he left, he went into commerce and learnt the leather-goods trade at a company which, at the time, held the royal warrant for Her Majesty the Queen, who is the Queen Mother today.

Some time later, he founded his own company, manufacturing handbags and personal leather goods for such prestigious British brands as Mappin & Webb, Asprey and Russell & Bromley. The company later received the royal warrant to Her Majesty Queen Elizabeth II for handbags.

In 1991 the Queen accepted a visit to the Launer factory to see how her bags were made. Unexpectedly, she spent the whole afternoon there, meeting the craftsmen and women.

J U D I T H   L E I B E R

F R O M   B A G S   T O   R I C H E S

Judith Leiber's life has all the makings of a Spielberg movie. Born in 1921 to an upper middle-class Jewish family of jewellers in Budapest, Hungary, she won a place at King's College, Cambridge, to read chemistry. Her studies were cut short by the Second World War, which prevented her returning to England after visiting her family in Hungary. By various twists of fate, her family escaped the concentration camps during the Nazi occupation. Her mother and sister would dirty their faces and don babushkas, pretending to be old women in order to avoid the unwanted attention of German soldiers. Judith joined the Hungarian Handbag Guild as the first-ever female apprentice and was kept busy cooking glue and sweeping floors.

One day in 1945, Judith bumped into a friend who was with an American GI, Gerson Leiber. A year later she married him and moved to New York. Judith worked for several handbag manufacturers before eventually plucking up enough courage to start her own business in 1963. Although she makes

day bags – albeit very expensive alligator ones – she is more famous for

her evening bags, which are covered in anything up to 10,000 Austrian

crystal rhinestones. The bags have been a favourite with America's First

Ladies, including Jackie Kennedy, Hillary Clinton, Barbara Bush

and Nancy Reagan (who gave one to

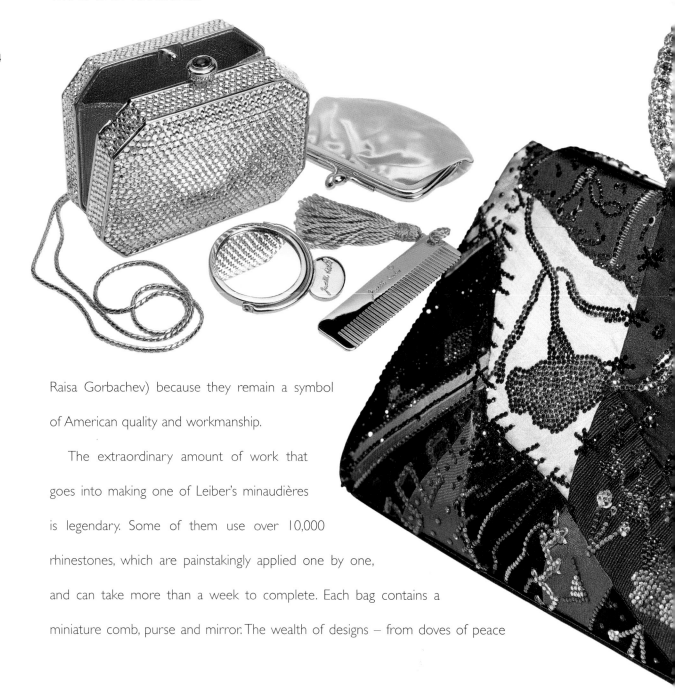

Raisa Gorbachev) because they remain a symbol of American quality and workmanship.

The extraordinary amount of work that goes into making one of Leiber's minaudières is legendary. Some of them use over 10,000 rhinestones, which are painstakingly applied one by one, and can take more than a week to complete. Each bag contains a miniature comb, purse and mirror. The wealth of designs – from doves of peace to mark the end of the Gulf War (*see below*) to rosebuds and polar bears – means the bags fast become collectors' items. In 1997 the Victoria & Albert Museum in London added one of Judith Leiber's Fabergé Egg bags to its collection. Not surprisingly, when Bernice Norman, from New Orleans, loaned her collection of 300 Leiber minaudières to the city's Museum of Art, a remarkable 10,000 people queued up to see them. Unlike most handbags, a Leiber creation can be guaranteed not only to serve a purpose to its owner, but to entertain those who surround her.

LOEWE
SOFT, SENSUAL AND SPANISH

The blueprint for Loewe style is supple, butter-soft leather made sexy. Although Loewe is sometimes called the Hermès of Spain, Enrique Loewe did not start out as a saddler. From the first day he started trading in 1846, out of his small shop in Calle del Tobo in the Spanish capital of Madrid, he sold small, exquisitely made handbags and accessories. By 1905 the King and Queen of Spain had become patrons, and their descendants, King Juan Carlos and his family, are still customers today. In 1947 Loewe became the sole distributor of Christian Dior's New Look clothing in Spain and only then became interested in designing a fashion line. When the company did so, in the 1960s, they specialized in creating flawlessly soft leather trousers, jackets and skirts in unusual but beautiful colours. The label has recently been given a refreshing injection of style by the appointment of Narciso Rodriguez to design the ready-to-wear collection in 1997.

L O N G C H A M P S
Q U I N T E S S E N T I A L L Y   F R E N C H

Walk along any street in France and you cannot help but spot fashionable women carrying Longchamp bags, known for being unpretentious and wonderfully useful, yet at the same time being rather smart and stylish. One of the most popular, the Pliage bag, is a folding nylon shopper that is trimmed in cowhide and has sold over a million since it was launched in 1994.

Founded in 1948 by Jean Cassegrain, the company originally specialized in leather-covered pipes. Over time the range was expanded to include humidors, ashtrays and pipe-holders. By 1970 Longchamps was producing a hugely successful nylon and leather luggage line. In 1998 the company celebrated 50 years in business with the 50th Anniversary bag, made in genuine crocodile with a lambskin lining and gold plate bamboo lock. There is no doubt that French women will snap them up.

118

MULBERRY
THE HUNTIN', SHOOTIN' AND FISHIN' BAG

Mulberry is all things English. The country squire style has been carefully cultivated by Mulberry's founder and designer, Roger Saul. Although Mulberry has the air of a company that has

been around for generations, it was actually established in 1969 when Roger started making chokers and belts based on horse tackle on the kitchen table of his flat. His girlfriend Monty, who later became his wife, was a model, and she successfully launched his designs by wearing them with very little else. By 1971 Roger had a staff of 16 craftsmen working in an old forge near Bath, using traditional leather-making skills.

The sportsmen theme has been carried through to both the fashion and the home collections, which are extraordinarily

successful in Japan and in the USA. By 1996, Mulberry was valued at £30 million. The popular, stylish Grand Despatch bag and Binocular bag, which bring a little of the countryside to the city, have both become modern classics.

OSPREY
A VILLAGE AFFAIR

After working in the fashion industry for some years, it was colour – or rather, lack of it – that made Graeme Ellisdon decide to set up his own company making belts and gloves in a full spectrum of lively hues and shades. He and his younger sister, Bain, taught themselves to plait, cut and stitch leather in a tiny room above a small barn in their home village of Kimpton in Hertfordshire, England. As orders grew, Graeme began to pass on his techniques to local villagers. The local craftspeople would drop by in the morning to pick up their work for the day then deliver it, once completed, in the afternoon. This kind of cottage industry was perfect for the high-quality, hand-finished product Osprey has come to represent. By 1990, Graeme had designed his first handbag, the small suede Tiffany, which was soon to be followed by the Dolly. He prefers not to use metal clasps, fastenings or trinkets so that the form of the bag is what catches the eye rather than the details. In his view, 'a woman likes to be perceived by the outward appearance of her handbag, but it is the contents that reveal what she's really like'.

PALOMA PICASSO
SEALED WITH A LOVING KISS

The daughter of Pablo Picasso and Françoise Gilot was born in Paris and named after the dove her father had designed as a symbol for the 1949 World Peace Congress. Growing up surrounded by art, Paloma too became an artist and designer. In 1980 she joined Tiffany & Co. where she created simple but stunning jewellery. Soon after, she worked on glass and china, fabrics and home furnishings, and even a signature scent and red lipstick. However, it was in 1987 that she created her first handbag collection, which showed her characteristic bold sensuous shapes and unexpected combinations, all inscribed with the kiss motif (see *above*). The kiss was born out of her first visit to London, when Paloma noticed that schoolgirls signed all their correspondence with Xs representing kisses. 'As a woman who works and travels a lot, I understand what my customers want and need,' she explains. And understand she does, as is testified by the people, such as Isabella Rosselini, Sigourney Weaver and Princess Masako of Japan, who carry her beautiful but very functional bags.

P R A D A
T H E I T A L I A N J O B

The black nylon zip bag with gilt chain handles captured the hearts of the fashionable post-1980s crowd, who were tired of the flashier designer bags and hungry for something new. Nylon was the antidote: it was anti-fashion — both industrial and modern — but was made desirable and reassuringly expensive in the form of the Prada bag.

Since 1913, the Fratelli Prada had been making luggage and handbags for the well-to-do Milanese. Their shop near the Duomo was fitted with mahogany and brass fittings made in England. The family business was founded on excellent products, but nothing in the range was particularly exciting. When Miuccia Prada joined the company in 1978 as a designer and shareholder, she decided to turn tradition on its head and make the company more a reflection of her own uncompromising and eclectic style, which can be described as rich bohemian. She loves

combining luxury with the unconventional and adding a little humour. This is seen in her Miu Miu range, where the best-selling bags are a squashy cow-print sack bag and a simple square sequin-covered bag. Each season, when the fashion pack descend on Milan for the fashion collections, editors and stylists rush to the shop to stock up on the latest shoes, boots and handbags. For international make-up artist Mary Greenwell, the shop is always her first port of call from the airport en route to her hotel. Along with Gucci, Prada has redefined Italian style, making it less *signorile* and more cutting edge than it has ever been. To the fashion cognoscenti, the *Borsa di Milano* (translated literally as the 'Milan bag') no longer means the Italian stock-exchange: it simply means Prada.

YVES SAINT LAURENT

CUTTING ABOVE

Yves Saint Laurent was born on 1 August, 1936, in Oran, Algeria, but left for Paris after his baccalaureate. He wanted to be a fashion designer and showed his drawings to Michel de Brunhoff, a director of *Vogue*, who used some of them in the magazine and who also introduced this young talented man to Christian Dior. Yves worked for Dior until his death in 1957, when he took over as art director at Christian Dior, and his first collection was a phenomenal success. In 1958 he met Pierre Berge, who became his business partner in 1961 when they formed the house of Yves Saint Laurent. His 'smoking' jacket for

women has become a classic

design, and he was the first designer

to be honoured by an exhibition at the

Metropolitan Museum of Art in New York in

1983, organized by ex-*Vogue* editor, Diana

Vreeland. Modernity through timelessness

is the key to his much-copied designs.

KATE SPADE
INSIDER INFORMATION

The criterion for a Kate Spade bag is, 'if it will be out of style tomorrow, it won't be added to the line today'. Kate's sage words are the fruit of five years' experience working as fashion accessories editor of *Mademoiselle* magazine, from 1986 to 1991. The experience made her realize that there were not enough no-nonsense bags with a sense of wit and propriety, so she set about solving the problem with her husband Andy Spade. Naturally, both the press and public fell for her light, nylon bags in easy shapes and have been enchanted by her more unusual designs, which draw inspiration from sources as diverse as beach umbrellas, Harris tweed coats and childhood memories. Six basic nylon shapes exist today, and although they are copied mercilessly, the real thing is distinguished by the black-and-white label. The logo is true to Kate's simple style and practical designs, which is exactly why modern women love the bags.

TANNER KROLLE

KEEP THE CHANGE

Tanner Krolle is changing. This discreet British company has been making classic leather goods for the past 140 years, but only in the last few years has it decided to reposition itself as an international, contemporary leather accessories brand. The new identity has been created by the design team, called 'the Partners', who were briefed to keep the company's strong heritage and apply a modern slant to everything from the stationery to the shop. The new Tanner Krolle woman is 'aged between 25 and 45, she's urban, independent, successful, confident, stylish, sensual, intelligent and elegant . . . appreciates quality . . . and wants a bag that isn't a badge . . . rejects anything flashy'. The designer brought in to work with this exacting brief was Kathy Formby, an American woman who had previously designed for Ralph Lauren, Calvin Klein and Tiffany & Co. Her first success was the Two-in-One Circles and Squares bag, which is now in its third season, and the Three-in-One Frame

bag, which has a removable suede clutch or shoulder

bag to take you into the night.

J P TOD'S
ONE MAN AND HIS MARKET

J P Tod does not exist, but if he did he would be smart, preppy and WASPish. The name, the brand and the idea are a marketing dream thought out and researched by the Diego Della Valle Company of Italy. This company was set up by Dorino Della Valle, Diego's father, in the 1940s in the Ascoli Piceno region and was primarily concerned with shoe design. Some years ago it created new brands, including Tod's, Hogan and Fay – all of which have been successful, but especially Tod's. The rubber-studded driving shoe became a classic worn by the well-to-do and the fashion cognoscenti the world over. Despite the increasingly difficult economy in Italy, the group has performed extraordinarily well, with the Tod's brand leading the way. Professor Michael Porter of the Harvard Business School used the company as an example of

corporate excellence. Naturally, handbags, belts and small accessories were to follow. International recognition was achieved in the first year the J P Tod's handbag collection was launched. The simple tote bag decorated with studs (*see right*) has become an instant classic, carried by Uma Thurman, Princess Caroline, Naomi Campbell, Catherine Deneuve and Kristin Scott Thomas. East and West Coast parties were held in September 1998 to celebrate the opening of 22 Tod's handbag boutiques in major cities in the USA – quite something for a man who does not exist, except in our imaginations.

TOP LEFT: **ACTRESS SARAH JESSICA PARKER**

VERSACE
ROCK STARS AND ROYALTY

134

Gianni Versace will always be remembered for bringing Hollywood glamour back to the catwalk and creating dresses that could launch careers, like that of Elizabeth Hurley. Born in southern Italy, which was known in antiquity as 'Greater Greece', Gianni chose the head of the mythical figure Medusa to be his company's logo because it represented 'the beauty and almost fatal fascination of the classical Greek tradition'. But the logo went on to represent the glamour and hedonism of the rock 'n' roll lifestyle Versace customers aspire to. His Medusa bag with studs, from his autumn/winter 1992–3 collection, was carried by Madonna, Sharon Stone and Barbara Streisand, and his Marilyn print bag, with handles made from costume jewellery, found favour with supermodels and inevitably became a collectors' item. His

friendship with Diana,

Princess of Wales,

who attended his funeral

in 1997, prompted the Lady Diana bag

in 1995. He famously said he liked to dress egos

and that those who did not have big egos could

forget it, which is probably why you will find

his handbags on the arms of personalities

like Courtney Love, Demi Moore

and Meg Matthews.

LOUIS VUITTON

TRAVELLING RIGHT

Now that it is possible to circumnavigate the world in not much more than a day, appreciating the implications of travelling 150 years ago is difficult to do. In 1852 when Napoleon became Emperor, France was blossoming and opulence had come into fashion. The full gowns women wore had to be carefully packed and laid away when they travelled, and master trunk-makers were commissioned to design custom-built pieces for just that purpose. It was to one of these men that a young Louis Vuitton apprenticed himself, and in 1853 the 33-year-old Louis became the Empress Eugenie's favourite. A year later he opened his own shop. He quickly began to design his own

RIGHT: **PR 'IT' GIRL MEG MATTHEWS, WIFE OF NOEL GALLAGHER**

canvases, but his striped and chequerboard patterns were soon imitated, so in 1896 he stopped using geometric lines and came up with the four-point star that is used today.

Despite the vagaries of fashion, Louis Vuitton adapted his trunks and suitcases to suit the age of the transatlantic steamers, the

great rail journeys and the advent of aeroplanes, and they remain the *sine qua non* of luggage for the sophisticated traveller. To celebrate 150 years, the company asked several fashion designers to create their own bag, with surprising results, such as Vivienne Westwood's bum bag (*see overleaf, top right*), Romeo Gigli's amphora bag and Helmut Lang's dinner-jacket case. Vuitton prides itself on never refusing special one-off requests, however unusual.

140

VIVIENNE WESTWOOD

COSTUME DRAMA

Vivienne Westwood knows no fear. In the clothes she designs and in her personal life she has done everything her own way, sometimes shocking but always enthralling both adoring fans and 'tut-tutting' onlookers. Westwood's first shop in the King's Road, London, sold 1950s-inspired clothes and memorabilia when the rest of the world was enjoying a hippie love-in. By 1974 she had moved on to clothing influenced by sadomasochism and the shop name was changed to Sex. She and her partner, Malcolm McLaren, were prosecuted under the obscenity laws, but that only seemed to encourage them and together they pioneered the anarchic Punk movement. When their relationship and design collaboration ended in 1983, Westwood proceeded to wow the fashion world with her mini 'Crini' collection, paired with skyscraper platform

shoes. By 1987 her re-worked eighteenth-century corsets were 'must-haves'. Her love affair with the art and fashion of the past is evident in all her collections, but is translated with a new perspective. At the 1998 launch of her first perfume, Boudoir, Westwood presented the journalists with a mini Gladstone-style handbag made in a pink toile de Jouy canvas and trimmed in gold leather. The bag epitomized her highly feminine ideals and designs. Wherever – in terms of time and place – her inspiration comes from, her orb motif always identifies her work.

Aigner
119 New Bond Street
London W1Y 9AB
0171 499 4041

Bill Amberg
10 Chepstow Road
London W2 5BD
0171 727 3560

Cartier
175–6 New Bond Street
London W1Y 0QA
0171 408 5700

Chanel
19–21 Old Bond Street
London W1X 3DA
0171 493 3836

Coach
8 Sloane Street
London SW1X 9LE
0171 235 1507

Connolly
32 Grosvenor Cres. Mews
London SW1X 7EX
0171 235 3883

J & M Davidson
60 Sloane Avenue
London SW3 3DZ
0171 584 1779
Designer handbags.

Dior
22 Sloane Street
London SW1X 9NE
0171 235 1357

Fenwick
63 New Bond Street
London W1A 3BS
0171 629 9161
Stockist of many designer
handbags, including Hervé
Chapelier, Longchamps
and Orla Kiely.

Ferragamo
24 Old Bond Street
London W1X 3DA
0171 629 5007

Gucci
33 Old Bond Street
London W1X 4HH
0171 629 2716

Lulu Guinness
66 Ledbury Road
London W11 2AJ
0171 221 9686

Angela Hale
5 Royal Arcade
28 Old Bond Street
London W1X 3HD
0171 495 1920
Vintage and antique
handbags.

Nathalie Hambro
63 Warwick Street
London SW1V 2AL
0171 976 5356
By appointment only.
Please phone for stockists.

Harrods
87–135 Brompton Road
London SW1X 7XL
0171 730 1234
Stockist of many designer
handbags, including Celine,
Hervé Chapelier, Fendi, Judith
Leiber, Launer Longchamps
and Paloma Picasso.

Harvey Nichols
109–125 Knightsbridge
London SW1X 7RG
0171 235 5000
Stockist of many designer
handbags, including Hervé
Chapelier, Fendi, Paloma
Picasso and Kate Spade.

Hermès
155 New Bond Street
London W1Y 9PA
0171 499 8856

Samantha Heskia
0171 589 9777
Please phone for stockists.

Anya Hindmarch
15–17 Pont Street
London SW1X 9EH
0171 838 9177

Donna Karan
19 New Bond Street
London W1Y 9HF
0171 495 3100

Calvin Klein
55 New Bond Street
London W1Y 9DG
0171 491 9696

Judith Leiber
0171 416 4160
Please phone for stockists.

Liberty
214 Regent's Street
London W1R 6AH
0171 734 1234
Stockist of many designer
handbags, including Barbour
and Hervé Chapelier.

Loewe
130 New Bond Street
London W1Y 9FA
0171 493 3914

Mulberry
41–2 New Bond Street
London W1 9HB
0171 491 3900

Osprey
11 St Christopher's Place
London W1M 5HB
0171 935 2824

Prada
44–7 Sloane Street
London SW1X 9LU
0171 235 0008

Yves Saint Laurent
137 New Bond Street
London W1Y 9FA
0171 493 1800

Selfridges
400 Oxford Street
London W1 1AB
0171 629 1234
Stockist of many
designer handbags.

Tanner Krolle
38 Old Bond Street
London W1X 3AE
0171 491 2243

J P Tod's
35 Sloane Street
London SW1X 9LP
0171 235 1321

Gianni Versace
34–6 Old Bond Street
London W1X 3AE
0171 499 1862

Louis Vuitton
17–18 New Bond Street
London W1Y 9MF
0171 399 4056

Vivienne Westwood
44 Conduit Street
London W1R 9FB
0171 439 1109

INDEX

ACKNOWLEDGEMENTS

144

The publishers would like to thank the following sources for their kind permission to reproduce the pictures in this book:
The Advertising Archives 17br, 19, 23, 78tr, 87br, 89br, 89tl, 90tr, 136, 138–9
Aigner 68
Bill Amberg 69, 70
J Barbour & Sons Ltd 25bl, 54br, 71
Jason Bell 89tr
Camera Press/Imapress /Stephane Benito 38tr /Richard Open 40/Rota 47l
Carlton Books Ltd/Patrice de Villiers 1 (Lulu Guinness), 2 (Gucci), 4 (Thierry Mugler), 7 (Lulu Guinness), 8 (Angela Hale collection), 30 (Hermès), 48 (Gucci), 55, 58tr, 59–63, 64 (Anya Hindmarch, Kate Spade), 88, 100tr, 111br, 128–9, 142
Cartier Ltd 56tl, 72–3
Celine, Paris 54tl, 74–5
Chanel 29bl, 78bl, 78br /Alvaro Canovas 76bl /Stephane Ciceron 56tr, 76tr/Laurent Herail 77b /Karl Lagerfeld 79
Hervé Chapelier 57tl, 80–1
Christie's Images 12br
Coach 82–3
The Condé Nast Publications Ltd 46r/Paul Bowden 92bl, 106/Coopers 140 tr/Clive Corless 92bc/Arthur Elgort 10, 50/Robert Erdmann 66 /Olberto Gili 125tr/Andrew Lamb 122bl, 123, 125l /Mark Liddell 122tr /Raymond Meier 125br/Sid Pithwa 124tl/Rapid Eye 140bl/Claus Wickrath 26l
Connolly 84–5
Corbis-Bettmann/UPI 36tr, 39
Christian Dior Couture 86, 87tl

Justin Downing 124br, bc
Mary Evans Picture Library 12, 13tl, 15/Bruce Castle Museum 14br/Fawcett Library 13
Salvatore Ferragamo 91
The Ronald Grant Archive 24br
Gucci/Raymond Meier 92br, 94br, 95/Mario Testino 93
Lulu Guinness 56cl, 96–7
Hermès/Frederic Dumas 41c, 100cl, 101, 102tl, 103
Samantha Heskia 99
Anya Hindmarch 56br, 104–5
Hulton Getty Images 16, 17tr, 18, 20, 21, 37tl
Orla Kiely 107
Calvin Klein 108–9
The Kobal Collection 16br, 24, 35
Launer 110, 111tl
Judith Leiber 57br, 112, 113r, 114–15
Loewe 116
London Features International Ltd 36bl, 46l/Craig Barritt 42br/David Fisher 43br /Gregg De Guire 43bl/Phil Loftus 52/Colin Mason 42bcr, 43c/Kevin Mazur 47r /W McBride 43clb/Denise Van Tine 27br/Williams/ Legge 42tcr
Longchamp 117
Mirror Syndication International 43tr, 77tl
Christopher Moore Ltd 26r, 27, 28, 29r, 94tl, 134r, 135l
Mulberry 34, 58bl, 118–19
Osprey 120
PA News 37br, 38bl, 53 /Barry Batchelor 45cr/Neil Munns 32
Paloma Picasso 121
Pictorial Press 25br/Jeffrey Mayer 45r/Zuma Miller 44tr
Retna Pictures Ltd/Craig Barritt 46c/Steve Chys 113l

/Bill Davila 43tl, 44 l, 102r /Steve Granitz 27l, 41r, 42bcl, 42tl, 42c, 42bl, 45l /King Collection 22/Larry Lazlo 44br/Brent Moore 42tr/Theodore Wood 43cr
Rex Features Ltd/Steve Fenton 137r
Yves Saint Laurent 127/Rive Gauche 126
Sotheby's Press Office 98
Tanner Krolle 54tr, 130–1
Telegraph Colour Library/ Benelux Press 144br
J P Tod's 54bl, 132–3
Topham Picturepoint 41bl
Versace 134bl, 135tc, 135br
Louis Vuitton, Malletier A Paris 14tl, 137bl, 138bl
Vivienne Westwood 141l/Nial McInnery 141tr
Front Cover: Kate Spade (Carlton Books Ltd/Patrice de Villiers)
Endpapers, front: Kate Spade (Carlton Books Ltd/Patrice de Villiers); back: Carmel Allen (Fab & Ram)

Every effort has been made to acknowledge correctly and contact the source and/or copyright holder of each picture, and Carlton Books Limited apologizes for any unintentional errors or omissions, which will be corrected in future editions of this book.

Special thanks are due to Deborah Fioravanti, Gianluigi Parenti at Prada (London), Caroline Kemp at Time Products PLC, Paula Snow at Connolly, and everyone who kindly supplied images for this book.

I am indebted to all the companies mentioned in this book whose wonderful PR directors have kindly provided valuable information and visuals. Thanks also to those who have helped me along the way, in particular Katie Sharer, Martha Delap and especially Dominic Drew. For the historical part of the text I must credit and thank Enid Nemy for her informative words in the book *Judith Leiber: The Artful Handbag*, the Victoria & Albert Museum for its wonderful collection, and Bill Amberg for his insight. I am also grateful to Venetia Penfold for asking me to write this book and to Alexandra Shulman, my editor at *Vogue*, for allowing me to do so.

Carmel Allen